Beginner's Guide To Learning How To Be An Entrepreneur
Let's Begin Your Journey w/ Some Inspiration

Shameka C. Carter

Beginner's Guide To Learning How To Be An Entrepreneur

Let's Begin Your Journey w/ Some Inspiration

Shameka C. Carter

Let's Begin Your Journey

As a new Self Published Author I have been asked many times how did I do it? So, I decided to create this Beginner's Guide for those out there who are looking to become an Entrepreneur. Not just an Author. The tools and guides provided throughout this journal is to help you tune into your mind deeply and mentally. To help you begin and see what it is that you really want. What and how you can begin. Knowing your WHY is very important. I hope this guide helps you to bring much Clarity and Understanding to your New Journey.

This is my way of giving back, thanking God and all the people the Universe has channeled to me through my journey. Remember a life of gratitude brings confidence, a positive outlook on life, and general well-being. Through this guide you will also experience your spiritual and physical/material benefits to you. As you go along, you will be reminded of many things discussed throughout the journal. Helping you develop an essential attitude and how to express this on a daily basis for your New Journey.

The Beginner's Guide is not just for the moment, but for Every moment through life!

Let's Begin Your Journey

I Am Perfectly Imperfect

I have problems & I'll be the first to call them out;
Yea, I get lonely cause lately friends & family don't stick around.
But I keep my hopes up because that's the one thing I can control;
I Don't fill my mind with petty lies & let that go.
And all my Troubles in my life Won't bring me down;
And all the Struggles in my life they Teach me how.
How I'm Perfectly Imperfect & when it hurts I just remember there's a Purpose;
I may cry today and smile tomorrow
& those nights I'm all alone,
Feeling defeated and beaten;
Abandoned and far from home,
I'll sit in silence and watch as the world moves along.
Looking at my hands, like I see puzzle pieces in my palm, wondering what the hell I did wrong.
I remember, there is a Purpose, all the walls I broken through;
I am Perfectly Imperfect, I smile for all those who help hold me up.
When the weight is just too much & I can't bare it all alone;
Oh, I'm Perfect & this world is Imperfect.
I am Human & Strong with much Purpose.
I'll Never be left Alone! So I'm Not sorry nor am I wrong.
I am a Person struggling to get through this inhumane world.
All My Struggles & Troubles will Rise me Up!
I Am Perfectly Imperfect!

Let's Begin Your Journey

Self Expression is Important

This is for you! This is your Safety Net.
Whenever you feel like writing, write down your thoughts.
They are Yours and You have the rights to them.
Self Healing Begins Within.

Investing in Yourself: Beginners Tips

Creating your goals is not as easy as you may think. At the same time, of course it is possible and you can & you will do it. Let's learn some great tips to help put things into perspective for you.

1) Before you act, know what it is you exactly want. That must be your main focus.

2) Ponder. Think about your goal carefully, especially before making any major decisions.

3) Always remember this is a Goal that you want to set so it has to matter just as much as anything else. You have to want it as much as you want to breathe.

4) Think. Always THINK about your goal. It should be your baby. You wake up thinking about it. Go through your day thinking about it and go to sleep thinking about it. Everyday write down your goal.

5) Relax. Now this is where you are probably like, "Why relax?" Being relaxed helps clear the mind and when that is accomplished, you will be able to then put many things into perspective. So, yes RELAX. Stress will never do you any good.

6) The three F's. Family, Fitness, Faith, & Finances. Those are all four major things that will be a part of your goal. Quick breakdown. You have family you care about so they are/should

be taken into consideration. They will be there with you along this journey.

7) Fitness. You must be healthy to conquer your goal. Therefore it is important to try and stay healthy no matter the cause. You will need much energy and a straight mind. Never Lose Sight Of The Fact You Are Doing Something To Be Better!

8) Faith. Have faith in YOURSELF & your Goal. STOP the excuses. The time you spend sitting on your phone, in front of the TV or hanging out can be time spent on Your Goal. Every second you spend matters.

9) Finances. Yes, this is a tough one. How will I be able to finance what I want to achieve when I have Life already overwhelming me? That is true. Sacrifices. Cut back on things you use to waist money on. Partying, spa day, unnecessary essentials, shopping when not really needed, ect. Yes, those things matter.

10) Get a NOTEBOOK. That is how you begin writing down all your plans. Your thoughts. Planning things out. All of the above. Writing with pen and paper is most important. Why? It is repetitive. It is you repeating the thoughts in your head which is what you want and need. Make sure it becomes a matter of course throughout your day.

All of these tips are just beginner's thoughts. It's a lot right? If it's in your heart, soul and mind, nothing will alter your goal. It will not be handed to you. THIS IS NOT A MANUEL. It's information. You must do the work. So, begin the work. Because it is work. You will lose a lot. You will have many sacrifices to make. You have to choose if it is worth it to you.

Let's Begin Your Journey

A World of Understanding

In this world you don't get to know the WHY'S, it just IS.
Some may think it is an illusion, but a moon smiles;
It can be while in motion and it flowing through the clouds,
It still shows a smile to show you its Light;
Maybe to signify that it is simply a brighter night.
A full moon isn't always meant to be a bad sign;
Our minds are transmitters, so if we change that, the sign changes.
Like a sparkle in a diamond depends on the flaws in the diamond;
This world is full of flaws and nor is it ever going to be perfect.
But You can make your own world Perfect for You;
See things however you want to see them.
Drifting away is, like the wind in a storm that appeared out of nowhere;
Your perspective on life can spring upon you just like that as well.
In life you can get through anything, as long as someone has your back;
Sometimes, just to be there to Listen, that's all.
Everyone doesn't have someone to have their back, but there is always away to be heard;
Never keep your silence no matter what because our voices need to be heard.
Life can feel like you are living a Life Sentence;
Actually, we are all just experiencing a world that was created for us to create our own World.
One day things will all make sense and fall into place;
For once, you will be so happy to be alive creating Your world.

Do You Want To Preserve Your Good Within?

Let's Begin Your Journey

You Can & You Will

Let's Get Started On Your Ten Goals!

What are your Top Ten Main Goals? We all have more than one goal right? So, in this task you will learn how to format your goals from your Main Goal down to your Short Term Goal. Everything comes down to priorities and what you would like to accomplish in the end. Here you will get ideas on how to strategize your Ten Goals. Let's Begin :)

1) What is your main Objective for your goal?

2) Why do you choose that goal? (Think Very Hard)

3) How will you incorporate your goal within your family?

4) Decide how you can accomplish your fitness plan within your day. Even if it means waking up an hour early for a 30 minute workout. Remember the FOUR F's:
(Family-Faith-Fitness-Finances)

5) Where does the Faith come in place for your goal? (Ex: It can be prayer, meditation, even part of your workout & better, Remembering to write down your goals.) That gives you much Faith.

6) Figure out what works best for you to Educate yourself on that Goal everyday. (Read about it, watch a video, communicate with another entrepreneur, ect.)

7) What is it that you want your goal to bring to others?

8) How can your goal influence your family to make them feel engaged?

9) How will you manage to work on your goal and still live your daily life?

10) What is your aspiration for your Main Goal?

These 10 goals are to help you have a clear understanding of achieving your Goal. Remembering your goal everyday is part of becoming an Entrepreneur. A task you can do is make sure everyday you write down these Goals. They all contain your MAIN GOAL. They are important. There are no excuses in wanting Real success in life. Do the task and have fun with it. If you don't put in the hard work, you can not expect great results.

Remember This Is For You. Always Be Mindful Of That.

Control the paradigms. When you change the paradigms, you're changing how you think about something. Do not postpone your ideas.

Let's Begin Your Journey

Phenomenal Art Within

Standing in a crowd alone, looking around, heart racing, mind scattered;
Control your situation. You are in charge. But must one fend for themselves always?
For you are not. GOD, the higher power is right there with you;
One must think for themselves, for others may not think the same way.
Standing & thinking, One must protect Itself for others are indeterminable;
Moving along, slow this time. Mind resting. Watching others move afloat.
One knows the energy flowing from the imagine of self, one will no longer be scattered;
Nothing is visible but the moral seen far ahead.
Manifesting high principles for proper conduct! In Store this in your mind;
See the beauty in what one has and go with it. Hold onto it & never let it go.
It is now stored in the mind as data. Data that can only be processed by YOU;
You hold the master key to the process of this moment that once had you scattered.
One has now become one of the floating humans around itself but only now at a higher level;
Level of Control. One has grasped & mastered this confusion;
Obedient!! Obedient to one self! Submissive to its own will.
YES, one has Manifest & Conquered Obedience to One's self.
PHENOMENAL ART WITHIN!!!!

Time To Begin Manifesting Your Ten Goals.

In your Ten list of goals, which one is Your Game Changer? Which one is your Top? Write it down LAST but remember it's THE MAIN GOAL. So, with your list write down which steps you would take to get to Your main goal. Remember: Ponder, Think, Relax.

The Domino Effect

Can your Game Changer take you to help your other goals?

Go to your list of goals. Choose which one that can knock out all your other goals. The one that can take you to the others and land you to the Main Goal.

That's the goal you should begin with. Everything is a process. There are steps. You want the steps that will take you to where you are aiming for but growing along the way. Take you on many journeys which will also be very educational. You wouldn't even realize it. That is very important in the process of being an entrepreneur.

Now, that may have seemed so easy to you. You know how many people do not even think of the "Domino Effect" process? I'm sure you may not have. You become scattered because you are anxious and determined to just make your goal succeed. Understandable and that is okay. That is why we have guidance. We all have to start somewhere.

Becoming an entrepreneur is totally different than just trying to land that good ole corporate job. It's draining, stressful, time consuming, and hard work. Dedication and consistency is a major part. You still have your daily priorities. That is why having a list of goals and preparing the Four F's is an importance. Hope we are getting somewhere now. You are getting there :)

Let's Begin Your Journey

There Will Never Be A Last Day Without You

Light hits our face so bright, wanting you to just stay til night with me;
The warmth of your fingers, seeing forms of the trees, in the moment feeling so free.
The storm and the sea, the sun is rising and then will set;
Day's maybe long, as our hearts beat as one, a moment I'll never forget.
Til the day were done, until the sky has no sun, and the day we just begun;
We will forever see the sunshine in each one.
Trying to not allow the night to end, but watching the sun arise upon the sky;
Together we sit here in our moment we will never forget, wondering why we question the why.
Taking chances to be free in the moment, accepting this feeling of content;
This thing is too big to fail, so don't change what is probably meant.
Trying to not let things get the best of us wishing they weren't true;
Don't look if you don't want to find, cause then we may miss what could have grown.
There is pain deep inside, are we truly willing to try;
For those old scars won't heal and they won't conceal.
For those old scars will refuse, but they will win and we will lose.
Can we fight together, heal within and learn to love above;
No words to describe what we feel, but what we do know is we have Love.
Nothing but action to change the pass,
Lord, wondering can we fight this mass?
I know I want nothing but to show and prove more trust;
In my heart and soul, I know for you and I as well, that is a must.
For what we have conquered and still remain, I am honored to still remain.

Let's Begin Your Journey

Can You Love? Do You Know How To Love Yourself?

What Is Your Why? Your Reasoning.

1) Who: Who are you doing this for? No one can answer this for you and this question is not easy. You probably would have said for yourself, your family. THINK of what your goal actually is. THINK.

2) What: What is it that you want from accomplishing your goal? Main objective to how this became about. INTERNALLY, what is it that you want to accomplish from this goal?

3) When: Now, you have to have a plan. What is your ideal timing to land your goal? Through your Ten List, think about the possible logic timing of those goals. Then think of when you want to have your goal set. Pressure? Yes, that's part of the process. There will be much pressure. DEADLINES! When?

4) Where: Within your goal, where would you like for it to take you? Where do you want to be? Where do you want your goal to land you?

5) Why: Why did you choose this goal? Only you can answer that.

May some of these things seem similar, get used to it. Once you reach your goal, that will be the same thing. REPETITIVE. You will be doing the same things over & over for a while. You will have to network and speak. This is helping you get used to it.

Let's Begin Your Journey

The Pass vs The Present

It feels so real, like I can feel a bullet going right into my chest,
Sometimes life can get real dark & it gets kind of hard to tell the difference between reality & a nightmare.
We keep dreaming like we are relapsing & it feels very real,
You see, we have chances in life & we need to use them while we can.
We are all so stuck in the past, we still trying to figure out how to run away,
Trying to do anything so we can stray.
Closing our eyes & trying to envision something different,
But when our eyes open, we're still stuck with Ourselves.
So, every morning wake up & pray to your higher power for help to accept the things we can't change & courage for the things we can.
Can't run away from our past, it's a part of us, it's what makes us who we are.
The darkness & nightmares, we gotta lock that away because it isn't real, & it'll hurt us only if we let it leave us scared.
Minds need to be structured & focused.
Now is the time to change & make a New Life.

Can You Plan To Leave The Past Behind? You Deserve To Move Forward.

What Makes You Comfortable Can Break You.
What Makes You Uncomfortable Can Make You.

Learning pressure and time limits is important. It's a great attribute to your journey. You should be nervous about starting a new endeavor in your life. If you don't then there is no challenge. Where is the time to fall or make mistakes? That's what will cause you to grow and learn. Challenges, you must yearn for them. If you feel scared and uncomfortable, it means something isn't right. It's a saying and you must take Risks and leave the Fear behind. You lead with fear, you will overcome many things.

These things will help you a lot. A key to many things in life is Listening. Take in as much information as you can. Pay attention and apply it. You are the one who will be doing the work. You are the one who must learn all that one can. Be more knowledgeable about what your goal is so you don't end up going into many things with a blind folded eye.

If you have gotten to this point so far within this journal and have attended by actually writing, you have already Started. Do you see that? That is you presenting your dedication to your goal already. You have most likely identified your why. Congratulations on proving your ambition towards your future as an entrepreneur and reach your main GOAL!

OH, DON'T GET TOO EXCITED. THIS IS STILL THE BEGINNING :) LET'S KEEP IT ROLLING!

The Unexamined Life is Not Worth Living

How will you know who you are?
How do you figure out who you are?
Not just who you are, but deep inside who you are.
What's your strengths, weaknesses, what empowers you?
Cause you can make you who you are.
Can you interpret it, put it all together as one?
Make it YOU!
Yes it's difficult & maybe one of the hardest to do
Not many people have thought of this question in life.
Maybe, it could actually save so many things & most importantly,
People.
So, do you examine your life?
Because a life Unexamined is not worth living.
It will have destruction, confusion, and wrong paths.
Take the proper time & look at You.
Examine yourself, explore yourself.
It's worth your life; it's worth your own soul.
You must know Who You Are!
An Unexamined Life Is Not Worth Living!

Let's Begin Your Journey

Do You Know Who You Are?
Write It Down & Read It.

Why Question Who I Am?

It is important to always remember who you are. When you place yourself into a business setting, you REMEMBER who you are and why you are becoming an Entrepreneur. Why? In the business world, it's important because there will be times where you will have to step out of your comfort zone. That's the part where "What makes you comfortable can break you. What makes you uncomfortable can make you" comes in play. That may not be the case all the time. For example:

You are planning to run your own business but you still have to maintain your current lifes finances. You will have to network & know how to conduct yourself in business settings. You may have to meet with investors and you have to know how to WOW them. Just like you will have to engage with your supporters. This should come Naturally because this is your passion. So, why the task of asking "Do you know who you are?" If you go back to what you wrote down, ask yourself if it gives you the answers that would apply to this scenario.

Challenges! We must always challenge our own selves for the success we want so badly. We must be able to embrace being critiqued at times. Be Prepared For The Unknown Always. Know your Goal Completely, Know Your Why, Know Your Business Plan. It is Essential. I'm sure this all just made much sense to you as to why the prior tasks were asked.

THIS IS FOR YOU & WHAT YOU WANT! KNOW IT FROM THE BACK OF YOUR HEAD. EDUCATE YOURSELF ON IT IN EVERY WAY POSSIBLE. BE THE BEST AT YOUR GOAL!

Let's Begin Your Journey

When You Are TALL, You Are The Person They See

Rising high in life, people will begin to notice,
Fighting through battles, people will notice.
There will be bad vibes and talks, which makes you important,
You don't get distracted, you remain focused.
In the end, you are all that matters, you are your success in the end,
Never wonder what another is doing or feeling.
It will distract you from your own light,
Everything in this world is up to you and your energy.
Cold sometimes, irrational, and yes angry at times,
But love beyond flaws, words and actions.
Light is always shining even in the darkest moments,
Never let it blind you, yes shining can cause distraction.
You bare it well and flow through your walks head held high,
For that shows strength and much ambition.
Heads will turn and attraction will follow, some not always good,
But you stay firm in your stance and the negative will eventually disappear.
Others will admire, some may adapt and follow the positive energy
And there you will see, That's how you Know you are TALL.
You have been SEEN remarkably!!

How Can You Make Yourself Stand Out?

Achieving Your Goal

1) Your Accountability Partner. Sort of like a mentor which is a great asset to have as well. You will meet with this person once a week. Choose a day and time that works best for you both. You will share your goals and tasks for that week. Every week you set a major task towards your goal. This person is there to push you, encourage you and give you the best advice. Choose your partner carefully. Why is this good? It no longer becomes just about you. You must now prove to this person that you will make this happen and they believe in you. Don't waste their time.

2) Plan in your daily task how much time in your schedule you can work on your goal. Best if you can map it out weekly.

3) Master commitment and structure your mind. Train it because now you have to build a platform. Social & Marketing.

4) Gain your audience by targeting Everything that has connections with your goal. Engage and put yourself out there. RISK. You don't know until you try. EDUCATE.

5) Saving money, cutting back on things so you can INVEST it in your Goal instead. Which is more important? A good investor knows that, It's not how much something costs, It's what it will be/is worth. EVERYDAY WORK ON THESE 5.

Rain Drops Falling

I lay and hear the sounds of dripping rain through my window,
Picturing the clouds and a slight darkness in my head.
It's early, but I'm so lazy to roll over and see what is the reality of what I hear,
Maybe it's just water dripping from my window shed from rainfall earlier.
Either way, the sound feels so relaxing and peaceful,
My body is numb in some sense as I lay and just hear the sound of the drops.
Positive thought of, "God is washing away as much ugly as he can through each drop."
Brings a smile to my face and energy to turn and look out the window.
To see tree branches leaning, a dullness in the sky,
Drops of water falling in front of me, as I remembered the pure feeling it gave me.
There was always beauty in rainy days for me.
Wanting to one day just stand outside in the street and let it pour on me,
Sit on the hood of my car and let it rain on me, and just smile, embracing this cleanse.
As I continued to watch in deep thought, I began to see the rain coming to an end,
Slowly but admiring the form of the transformation, seeing the sky slowly lighten up.
Was God waiting for me to turn and see this? To have me in my thought of awakening?
Either way, It gave me the strength to get up and start my day Joyfully,
Signs from the Lord, Pay attention to them More.

Let's Begin Your Journey

What Is My Start Up Plan & Do You Need Help?
"Remember Your Top Ten."

Your Start Up Plan..........

In your journey you will lose many people. Why? They will not understand your new ways. Simply, and bluntly people never really want to see another succeed before they do. There will come times where you will not be able to communicate with those that you are used to. Your way of thinking and daily routines will have changed. Your mindset and conversations are going in different directions. You can not control what others may think or feel about what You want for your future. Don't lose sight and Don't give up feeling bad that you are taking a new path in life. Doesn't mean you don't like, love or care for them. You just applied those to Yourself alot more. Selfishness! You need to be that in order for your Goal to begin.

You will experience many things. This is a life changing journey that you have chosen so be as prepared as you can. Many will doubt you. Many will tell you that you will fail. Remember that those people have probably/most likely never even thought of doing what you are trying to achieve. Or they have and never took the steps that you have so far. So, go out and meet people. Introduce yourself and network. You are your Goal now. Everything you do will represent that. You must find ways to make your goal part of you.

Let's Begin Your Journey

Walk Your Fate

Things always happen without warning. We question them, Why?
Take whatever has happened, good or bad, trade it for something More.
Maybe it will change your soul, heart, and mind;
No sense in drowning in thoughts, take action upon.
For all we as humans know, any and everything is undetectable;
But we have the will & the chance to turn things around if we Choose.
See, choices is a major concept in this world. Choices!
We have the ability to CHOOSE which way we want to turn & guide ourselves;
For we are not weak. No we are Not!
We all have that inner strength that can be tuned into;
Like a magician, magically making miracles happen.
So I ask, why waste time wondering, questioning, doubting & drowning our great souls: turn them into "Miracles"
Cause anything, good or bad, Can be turned around!
That is a choice we make, An ability we have.
Use It! Cause guess what, Nothing really happens without warning.
Walk Your Fate!!!

Let's Begin Your Journey

What Can Catch Their Eye?

Branding And Marketing

Remember while putting yourself out there, you must make yourself original. What makes you better than another? Marketing and Branding your business is essential. It's delicate like a flower. While creating ideas for your brand, do your Research. Amazing tip here. Look at what you are trying to pursue. Research it and see what works great for others and see how you can apply it to your brand. Make it more fascinating, good content. Make your customers/ supporters feel WOW. Make it memorable. They won't forget it and will tell others about an amazing Marketing/Branding presentation that they have seen or heard. Now, don't let presentation take you off guard. You Can accomplish this with your presence. How you speak about your business and present it. CONFIDENCE and using intriguing ways to express your brand. You are a Brand now. When you are branded you can charge double. You can offer other services. You EXPAND. This is why Branding and Marking is so important. This is how many make money before their business even takes off.

YES, you can make money for your business before it even takes off. You can catch your audience beforehand. It is all about catching their attention. What makes your business stand out? Branding and Marking is how you can accomplish that. They will want to work with you. Do the research and see what has been working for other companies similar. It's not copying. It's researching and learning.

Never Question Yourself

Sitting outside on the stoop, wind blowing, slight chills through the body;
Air is peacefully oddly cool, like a breath of fresh air. Enough to make you awaken.
Awaken to your reality. The one that was beginning to drift off;
Drift to a state of the mind that was once no longer of existence.
Pure, Real, Mind blowing, & Shocked, this just happened?
Caught myself, & grabbed my hold back on my strength!
Did I just find a way, a place to drift to, that felt nonexistent for afew?
Woah, what a pleasant feeling. I just managed that power.
Gave myself a perfect setting for an escape.
My mind hears water flowing, imaging waves glide across a bay;
The sound, I can hear it! So relaxing as I drift to this picture I created.
Feels as if I'm in with the tide of waves, fresh & purity;
I look up, glance at the clouds, seeing the sparkling stars gazing through the sky.
They are shining down on me as well, as I smile & say a few words to one;
Like a little girl, who wishes upon a star? I do & I am.
My soul feeling so free, so peaceful, in a place of my own serenity;
I can't allow this feeling to be taken away. It's too perfect & glorified upon me.
Something is being installed in me & I feel it through the cold breeze, even my cold fingers;
Can't deny what is for you. I repeat & repeat. I can not deny what is for ME!
Im changing, I want change, I feel change & it is right there for me;
Grab it, claim it, stay strong & defeat the evil. It is Your's. This change is Your's & You fight for it.
So, I look up at the star once again & say out loud, Never Question Yourself!

Let's Begin Your Journey

You Got This! Write Down What You Already Know.

What Is The Importance On This Journey?

It is extremely important to understand the limits of a business plan, particularly one that is early in the game. You will have to begin a start-up capital from individuals or a bank. Unless, you have the funding of your own. Either way, a written business plan will help you get your ideas across to perspective lenders and investors if needed. A vision board is a previsual business plan. Someone who is considering putting money into your venture will want to see your plan in writing.

This includes your business ideas. Why do you think it is a good idea? Your background, experience, contacts, where you plan to locate, how will you manufacture your inventory? How will you find and keep your customers? Do you know the status of your competition in your goal? How much money & you will need to start and break down into details. How much are you able to invest into your own plan? And how do you plan to repay the loan or investment?

Always proceed with caution, keep your eyes open, and let the experience be your guide. Not just a writing plan. Refer back to the task that was asked, "Who, What, When, Why." Things should start making sense. You should have this planned out already by this time. Especially with the information already given. YOU MUST DO THE WORK. These are just some tips/informative information.

Let's Begin Your Journey

No Understanding

As you sit and look at your surroundings you see;
You observe the things that are there.
Things that are right in front of you;
Some had no understanding at the time.
Confusion to what is being put in your path;
All we know as humans is what we are as a person.
We act upon what God has placed in front of us;
Many are very bling to what are right in front of us
All we know as humans is to who we are as person;
What we have been gifted with, to what we are as a person.
Why are we put in these situations? We don't know;
But we know who we are, If we know who we are!
See the good in the negative, even if it's not right.
Do God's work. Never decline the job he has given you!
Everything is not for everyone, in no way possible.
Stuck to what is in the presence of us, but can't be seen;
See this is what makes life so beautiful in such a rare form.
Glory in the light of so many things!

Let's Begin Your Journey

What Do You Know/Learned By Now?

Clear Understanding Of Your Circumstances.

Now what do you know already so far? You know your main goal and your short term goal. You have put many of your Ten Goals into some type of perspective. Some thoughts on Marketing and Branding. Now lets keep going and learn many more tips.

Many people will want to pay thousands of dollars to promote their business to start off. That's okay if you have the means to do so. Go for it. But some do not, so what do you do? There is always away. You will find one.

Social media platforms are a good way for marketing but to an extent. You may not always reach the audience you are looking for. Networking in person is the greatest way. You engage with people and they get to see who they would possibly be working with first hand. You give them the First Impression. Which is why the tasks on the journal writing were asked for.

You become comfortable with learning how to do this if you are familiar with it. Watch seminar videos, YouTube videos, read books, research your business and find what others are doing. Practice in a mirror. You will end up doing whatever it is that you have to in order to achieve your goal. Take that time throughout your day to educate yourself on that goal the best way you can.

IT IS ALL ABOUT MASTERING YOUR GOAL! YOU BECOME YOUR BEST TEACHER.

Life's Working Progress

Life is a working progress, wise people understand what this mean;
You must believe in yourself first foremost before anything.
You must admire your passion and put your best effort forward;
For you never know the power you have unless you try.
You glaze up into an empty air and you imagine yourself in a place;
A place more than what you are now, you grasp that and hold onto it.
Take yourself to that place and strive for it, don't give up!!
Understand that You are that prize of your goal and No One can take it from you.
We all have dreams, we all have wishes and desires;
How do we accomplish them? Dedication! That's the major key.
A mother, A father, have a child, they have dedication. An obligation;
There is no turning back, You have already presented this presence, existence.
Take your goals, dreams and desires into the same aspects as that concept;
You can not lose if you Never give up!!
May take longer than you desire or maybe quicker. It depends on You;
But great things always take time, effort, and dedication.
So remember, Life is a working process that you can master to Your Own!!

Let's Begin Your Journey

What's Your Progress So Far?

How Hungry Are You? Let's See…….

Have you figured out a strategy yet? Everyday, have you been writing down your ten goals? Remember you are supposed to be starting with your Short Term Goal. That goal will get you through all your other goals that will take you to the TOP GOAL. THE GAME CHANGER! This process was to apply pressure, training and structuring your mind. Keeping you focused on what you are aiming for. There is no need at this point to write down daily action steps because you have those planned out already. Focus on your goal and the others will follow up.

By now things should start making sense. Should not have any excuses and have some clarity on your goals one by one. Because you know what your WHY is. You know where you should begin and how to start working your way up. If not, don't worry everything takes time. The pressure that you may have felt during writing down your ideas in the task sections should have given you a push.

Vision Boards, Mediation, Faith, Prayer, Grateful, Motivation, Fitness, Being Proud of Yourself: Any or all those things will absolutely give you clarity and help reach your goal. Always stay dedicated and remember your WHY. Don't stray. There is no room for breaks in reaching your goal as a Business Owner. Being Your Own Boss.

SO HOW HUNGRY ARE YOU? REMEMBER THAT ALWAYS!

Turn Life Around For Your Will

Sun shines down like a glaze of sparkle off a shining glass;
Smiling at the image is the purity of earth's grace.
Trees with beautiful green leaves, some with floral colors;
Birds flying out of them, what a beauty and site to see.
This is Earth, very existing and in pure form;
Standing there admiring life's form, the sun beaming upon you so warm.
Looking around and you see people smiling, laughing;
Enjoying life, even if it's for that moment.
Joy felt in your heart and chills through your body;
Because this is the reality of a beautiful scene that most wouldn't see it as.
We all get peace and some calm in a day, just don't realize it;
Because you may be so caught up on the other side of life.
The other side where we have our burdens, trials, worries;
They will always be there because that is Life.
We take the good with the bad, and the happy with the sad;
How you interpret these things is how they will be conceived.
It's not supposed to be a breeze in the park, whats the glory in that;
Let it build you, make you stronger and wiser.
For everything we go through in life is for a purpose;
It is a choice to how we manage what is thrown at us.
Go back to the beginning, the bright sun, the smiles, the laughter;
It is still there, tone into that when those downs kick in.
Knock the Devil out the park, turn that negative into a positive.
You will see and have greater results, for all God has promised;
Trust in your will, your ability and your strength to over power the negative force.

Let's Begin Your Journey

What Do You Normally Gain Out Of Your Daily Life?

Now What Do You Want To Gain? You Know :)

Work, Stress, Bills, Time, and a Lifestyle. That is your normal. That is basically everyone's normal. That is what we are trying to eliminate and replace. But being a business owner does not totally eliminate these things. It is more work but it is YOURS atleast and something that you want and enjoy. You know your WHY. You should know by now.

All this is to help put things into perspective for you. It is necessary and very cooperative. Having a Mentor is a great asset. Now, I know we spoke of an Accountability Partner. That is the opposite. That is a person that you are personally engaged with and believes in your goal as much as you do. That is personal and you do not want to let them down. A Mentor is there to guide and help educate you through your process with knowledge.

A great tip to help you gain is to Invest. You are investing in yourself and your goal. Investing in the stock market, trading is a great part of the business world. It can help you achieve your goal. Sacrifices, cutting out things that are not really a necessity. Then you can really gain a LIFESTYLE. That trip you plan twice a year or even once a year, cut it short. Put that money to the side. Research and see what is going on in the stock markets. This may not be for everyone but as for Entrepreneurs it is most likely beneficial.

JUST TIPS & IDEAS TO HELP YOU GAIN MORE THAN YOU THINK YOU CAN!

Attraction of Life

Sometimes you just want to fall back in love with your old self;
Then realize it's the old you because it's to help you evolve into a better version of yourself.
I will always be there for those I love and care about because that's just who I am;
You must adore, admire and fall in love with yourself first.
Then you can come full circle with the universe and what's in it;
The greatest things that are meant will follow you.
Somethings are meant to be kept alone, kept to yourself;
Being open can drag a lot of negative energy towards your way.
Everyone is not here nor will be there for the best reasons;
You must kill off your demons and believe God is there for you.
Drinking and drugs are only temporary healing you from your Demons;
You must focus on the real issue and face it/them head on.
Because Reality will eventually catch up with you.
Children these day's think Life is not worth shit;
Why? Because of what they see around them.
Society can not change itself;
If WE change ourselves, then the world will begin to change one person at a time.
See, the Cause and Effect in that scenario? We change, we are guaranteed to touch one out of ten people.

Let's Begin Your Journey

How Will You Attract People To Your Business?

Excellent Ways To Get Customers.

1) Identify the clients you are trying to reach. It's easier to address a marketing plan to help you attract your customers.
2) Know your location/locations of your clientele. Where will your business fit in best at?
3) Know your business inside and out. Which we have already gone over. Remember your notes. (Hope you been writing them down)
4) Position yourself as the answer. (Your customer) How would you want to be convinced into a company? Put yourself in your customer shoes.
5) Networking through platforms such as social media, LinkedIn, creating a business page and website.
6) Build partnerships with others. Get the word out there about your business to those who are business owners as well. They can relate to your journey. You can learn tips from them. Be a mental note taker.
7) Stay consistent with your work. Keep pushing and pushing your business. The drive and ambition will draw people to you. Do not come off needy though. Be professional, casual and confident about it always. Have to be blunt here.
8) Offer discounts and promotions. Have to always start somewhere but keep in mind, never sell yourself short. Make it reasonable. You are beginning a business. You're trying to make money. Not spend what you don't have yet. BUILDING UP.

Just a few tips to help you get started. You will get it all figured out soon. Let's continue the ambition.

Beyond Black and White: Color

Colors, colors everywhere. Bright and vibrant, eyes wide in amazed;
Things are not always just Black and White if you can see beyond.
A world filled with so many things, things of all sorts;
But for sure it is filled with Beauty all around.
Even the Ugliest thing has Beauty in it; Wonder why?
All things have a Deep inner peace but can always be disturbed.
See through the Ugly and the Beauty shall appear;
Tuning into something much more can bring clarity.
Our minds is Power and we control the device;
Our eyes function in light reflection, Our minds function as the device.
Working both functions Together, what can we gather?
Eyes, which give vision, the Mind that collects what the eyes intake;
What does one see? The choice of Black and White or the Beauty of color.
Vibrant, Bright, Clarity, to see more than what one can interpret;
See it for what it is, what you choose. Beauty!
Clarity that has brought Color to the eye. Beyond Black and White.

Let's Begin Your Journey

Brighten Your Horizons & See Beyond.
What do you see?

Expand Your Mind & Think Outside The Box

1) What can you do that is original to help your business stand out? Remember, you are starting out fresh and you need to make a great impression.
2) Make sure you are clear about defining your business, product or service in a focused way that is easy for others to understand.
3) When beginning a business be mindful that it will take a lot of time. Find time everyday even if it's ten minutes.
4) Knowledge based on experience is so important to success. It is a powerful strategy to focus on one field (a piece of your business) and get good at it.
5) Managing your time is the key to structuring your work to suit your lifestyle. Your beginning a business so you most likely still have your job, family, and other priorities.
6) With planning you can build a work schedule that accommodates such personal considerations as the time of day you work best, whether you have children, and financially what you may need.
7) Tip: Lunch breaks, have your book/books that help educate you on business. There are many steps that need to be mastered. Always research!
8) Increase both your efficiency and your effectiveness. The difference between efficiency and effectiveness is: Efficiency is how well you do things. Effectiveness is getting things done. How can you increase your efficiency and your effectiveness? Think about it.

Seeing Surpass The Fog

A foggy night staring into the dark night sky;
Searching for a star, a bright star particularly.
But the fog is covering them all;
For those stars are there, they do exist.
Just keep looking and pick a space;
Trust your instinct & you will feel.
Stare at that spot and speak to that star;
Your wishes, Oh we have wishes.
Not even a fog can cover that thought;
Make your wish an extraordinary one.
One that you shall think is impossible;
It's okay if it's not, as long as you can see past the ordinary.
Smile, feel that, imagine it and embrace the foreseeing;
Trust your instinct. Trust is really the best feeling.
The fog does not exist as you are in that moment;
In your wish, that extraordinary one that is possible.
Relax and admire the momentum you are experiencing;
See, right there, you have escaped the reality into an amazing time that shall come.
You have Already been heard upon;
Past the fog & through a star that you could not see.
Cause You are that Existing Star; You Are That Wish;
You must make it a reality, You have the Ability too!
Seeing surpass the fog and through the eyes of Your own!

Let's Begin Your Journey

Has Things Gotten A Little Clear For You? By Now You Should Have An Understanding of YOUR Goal! How Do You Feel?

This journal was to grasp your intuition upon what you really want to do. To help you begin the stages of being an Entrepreneur mentally. Having understanding immediately. That's what intuition is. If you truly want to make your dream or a goal come to life, then this journal most likely helped you want it more. Look back at those pages where you should have placed your thoughts. Even if you wrote only a few words, it means that your mind was in it. You were already beginning your goal. How? You were acting upon your intuition and your mind was working on that goal along the way. So, congratulations to you. It is not over and you have much, much more work to do. You should absolutely be proud of the steps you have taken.

Now, if you have not written anything down in those blank spaces, PLEASE don't be alarmed. You have read and you have made it to this point. You are granted the opportunity of course to go back and refresh everything and still begin. See, this is the twist. We are given chances and choices. Doesn't matter when we act upon them. Some just need a little more information before doing so. That is not a bad thing. That is a great quality. Mindful though, you are striving to become an entrepreneur. We can always press restart. Tip: If we just do it the first time around and believe in Ourselves, you save yourself and Your Goal some time. It was just notes right?

Now, you can get a bigger notebook and begin EVERYDAY writing down steps, ideas, resources, tools and the things you know you want out of all of this. Everyday you CAN find ten minutes of your time to attend to your dream/goal. YES YOU CAN.

Lightbulb moment: When you accomplish your Goal, you will have no choice but to put in twenty fours of your time. So, you should just get used to it now.

Success is an amazing feeling when you accomplish them. Make no mistake, every success story is different. The one You are going for requires your speciality. Remember your WHY.

There is no, I'll start tomorrow.
Something went wrong, it's not my fault.
I can't do it. It's too much.
I don't / have the time.
People are lucky.

Listen, take the risk. Time is of the essence literally. Money can return but your time will not. Through this life be sure of it, you will take losses. You will fall and struggle. It's the ultimate test in this world. Will you give up? Will you make excuses? Will you allow those things to weaken you? Will you ALLOW OTHERS to bring you down or discourage you? If you have those thoughts, get rid of them if you are truly trying to succeed. Reality is Reality. Having a strong back bone is necessary very much so. You will lose people along the way. You will see people's true colors.

DON'T ALLOW IT TO STOP YOU! YOU GO ACHIEVE YOUR GOAL WITH ALL THE BELIEF AND FAITH YOU HAVE WITHIN YOURSELF. STAY LOYAL TO YOURSELF AND YOUR GOAL.

You will become what you believe. In the end, you have yourself. Yes, family and so forth, but you have YOU. Understand that part. They will call you crazy for it. Say your selfish even maybe. Just train your mind to remain calm and focused in every situation. But silent at times so you can hear your thoughts clear. Things will not happen overnight and just because you don't see results right away does not mean your process is not working.

Rule, Big Rule: NEVER COMPARE YOURSELF AND YOUR JOURNEY TO ANOTHER. For your journey is yours and yours only. Your focus shall always only be on you. You can learn from another, absolutely. Everyone has their own shoes to fill and we can not ever walk in another person's shoes. Fill your own and do it with diligence. Let it be more motivation. Never let anyone tell you, you can't.

Learn "Discipline." Every morning when you wake up and you know you have to get to that nine to five job on time because your life depends on it, so you make it happen. That's Discipline. Now apply that same energy for your dream. That simple ten minutes a day needs to be Disciplined. The mind wants a break but you want a dream/goal. NO BREAKS! NO EXCUSES!

Our minds are magnets. If we think of blessings consistently, we attract just that. We see everything in a positive form always, we will attract that. But if we think of problems and negativity often, we will attract just those. Make them no longer exist. Always cultivate Good thoughts and try to remain as positive as you can through Anything. Don't forget to be grateful for what you DO have. For that will help you to add to it all.

Let's Begin Your Journey

A Negative mind can Never give you a Positive life.

May this journal help you find your way through the beginning of your journey. I wish it has inspired you through positive and thoughtful mindsets put along through these pages. We all have a calling in life and sometimes we don't know when they will show. Maybe you being drawn to this journal is the universe calling you in. Maybe it is your time and it is presenting itself. For whatever it may be for you, mean for you, it is here. Nothing happens by mistake or accident all the time. Especially positivity.

I wish you all the best and I hope this has brought some bewildering ideas to you. We all have a part of us that is yet to be discovered. Many parts of us sometimes. So, be open and allow yourself to be free and discover those parts of yourself. I am sure they are something to be plastered on a beautiful canvas.

I wish you all the best of luck in whatever your beautiful hearts desire. There is a whole world out there filled with amazing new things. Go ahead and become a part of it. I'm pretty sure there is much space for new success and empowering people to share with many others.

Time to line up at the starting line and listen for that ring. OH, wait, you already had it. Go ahead and make it to the finish line. You will get there. **NEVER GIVE UP NO MATTER THE CIRCUMSTANCE.**

LET'S GO MAKE SOME SUCCESS STORIES SHALL WE ●

You can find books by this author on AMAZON & GOODREADS.COM

This Author is on social media platforms as a Health & Wellness Advocate/ Mentor inspiring many people all over the world. Her story is mind blowing and her spirit is very unique. Powerful and loving author that is true to herself and many others. A heart that spreads so wide, you will wonder how one does all of what she has. She still finds time, love, compassion, and generosity to share with many. She was found through her journey by MTAC Branding and is now working with RokuTV which launched with FoodyTV on Roku. She is a Media Executive/ Analyst and works with many clients, over 200+ all over the world helping them to accomplish their dreams and aspirations with her team MTAC. You can find all the information below.

Amazon Books: "My Children Saved My Life" English & Spanish
"There Is NO Life Without Struggle"
Instagram: @meekcarter_mylife & @warbattles_speakout
RokuTV Pages: @foodytv & @streetbeatztv
YouTube: meekcarter_advocate
Facebook: Facility Management Group LLC
Email: Facilitygroup1124@gmail.com

www.ingramcontent.com/pod-product-compliance
Lightning Source LLC
Chambersburg PA
CBHW070837220526
45466CB00002B/799